SEA OF GREEN

ROSANNE ELWORTHY

Library of Congress Control Number: 2024913539

ISBN
978-1-964393-74-2 (Paperback)
978-1-964393-75-9 (eBook)
978-1-964393-73-5 (Hardcover)

With all my heart, I dedicate this book to my dear husband, Alan. As we celebrate fifty wonderful years together, I am reminded daily of our blessings.

To our five children and their partners, who exemplify kindness and generosity in every action, and to our twelve grandchildren, the sources of our joy and the heart of our journey—thank you. Life with you is beautiful, and for that, I am eternally grateful.

Table of Contents

CHAPTER ONE

It Ain't OZ

"So Todo I guess we're not in Kansas anymore"… A very popular line from a very popular movie. Well, I've come very quickly to realize how Dorothy with her cute pigtails, bobbysocks and naive attitude felt as her house landed in the outskirts of "Oz." Maybe I should explain a little before I venture out to take you for this ride which is somewhat like Dorothy's.

You see, "Oz" was a grand place, a place where everyone would want to live, bring up kids in. It had a great looking palace, everything neat and clean, just like the people who inhabited this storybook utopia.

The outskirts of "Oz," well that was just a different story all together. The outskirts were filled with what you might call "want-a-be-ozites." These were the people who more than anything wanted to live in "Oz," although they also knew deep inside, it would never happen. So the spark had gone out of their eyes, the striving for something better had faded from the front part of their brains to where it sat now somewhere in the back of their minds so the hurt wouldn't be so bad when they felt that impossible feeling of getting nowhere in their very souls. The outskirts of "Oz" was so much bigger than "Oz" itself, but with a lot less power. You see, the people here did have a lot to say, but who really wanted to listen to these mostly uneducated and differently colored people? Would you? Think about it! The sad thing about all of this was that even these people didn't expect anyone to listen or care about them anymore. So they stopped asking - they stopped expecting - even their rights! Saddest of all, they thought God had forgotten them, so they forgot him!

Now, maybe I've never been to "Oz" or even the outskirts of "Oz." My house, to my knowledge, has never even flown! Heck, I've never even seen a tornado, and I have never had to pick up dirty papers after a dog named Todo! But, the people - I've come to know ever so well. Now like I said before, my house never flew. Instead it was a van, and we drove it. It wasn't the land of "Oz" or its outskirts, instead it was a place called Coast of Palms, Florida. With its palm trees and water fountains as you exited off the main highway, it said "WELCOME" and don't go any further "LIVE HERE." I guess we listened. We lived there a long time before we really every knew of the "other" people and how they lived. Now we were good Christian people, loved the Lord with all our hearts, and brought our kids up to do the same.

Sometimes while taking nice relaxing drives in the afternoon or early evening, we would pass these massive areas just covered with cabbage at the outskirts, and every so often we would see what looked like a scene from "Gone With The Wind." All these black skinned people hunched over moving at a very steady pace not ready to win a race, but not ready to stop until the sun quit first. The women with their hair tied in bandanas swinging machetes that were as long as their arm and weighing probably as much as them. These women swing these machetes with the same determination as the men. As they filled their crates, someone took it and swung it up onto the truck that was parked in the middle of this flat "green sea" of cabbage. All this was okay with me - after all, I lived in the South now, no longer in Boston where nothing was this flat unless it was a parking lot for a mall. No one picked anything, at least not cabbage. Apples, maybe and then you went to an orchard on a Sunday drive, and you paid for their privilege to pick these perfectly colored and perfectly formed fruits. These people though, that we saw off both sides of the road, we learned later, didn't do this for pleasure or because they liked it or even that they chose this or their life's work. They did it to survive, to live!

Well, I don't believe in accidental happenings. I believe all things happen for a reason, God's reason. I believe he has a way of directing your path and bringing you to a place where he needs you where his work has to be done. So even though we may have thought we were on a relaxing Sunday drive, we were being directed by God for His work. Our hearts were being softened, our minds were starting to work overtime, thinking of these people we saw. Who were they really? Where did they come from? What were they like? The questions went on forever. It was funny though how the scene would start to fade a bit as you'd go back to "Oz." We would return to our comfortable homes, our well-groomed landscaped lawns, a place where I didn't' have to search the bottom of my purse to see if I had loose change or a food stamp left over because my kids needed milk or food. The Lord is good though. He always has that perfect plan waiting in His time!

Mr. Noah

The phone rang early that morning in the middle of November. The weather was getting cool as it did just before Thanksgiving. You needed a sweatshirt and pants when you went out. In the mornings, the grass was wet with dew, and the steam came off the pool. It had to be filled every other day with a couple of inches of water, now that the pool water was warmer than the air. We had to put the heat on most mornings just to take that uncomfortable chill out of the house, so we could climb out from under our sheets, blankets, and our over-stuffed quilts, (all matching of course) out onto our plushly carpeted floors to boil our water for our hot tea, so it would be all ready when we got out of the hot steamy shower where we would also have waiting our over-sized bath towels with that "Downey" fresh softness!

My friend Fanny, who was calling, had the same routine I'm sure. Her call gave me a surprise, when I think now. I don't know why I was surprised. I always knew God worked in surprising ways. She wanted to know if we would be interested in brining clothes and food out to the migrant workers. Well, sounding a lot like Dorothy with that naive attitude in my voice, I asked "what migrant workers? Where?" Then her answer came, it was those people, the ones in the outskirts called Lumbell. They were the people of the fields, the people we always saw but the questions we had about them were never answered, but now I was about to find out for myself first hand. I was going to see them, hear them talk, look into the eyes that I could never see because they were always so far away. Was I ready? I said "Yes." Without a thought, I made a time for her to pick me up and hung the phone up. Now my mind began to race, I felt a little anxious, my stomach got that weak feeling in it, and I started to take action on them. I went to my husband, Alan, and asked him to come. He even wrestled with the idea a while before he said "yes." I got a hold of a babysitter for our then three children, the youngest being about ten months old.

Excitement started to get pretty high as we started out. After all, we were doing God's work - noting to it. Matthew 25 wasn't so hard, actually it seemed pretty fun so far! Clothe the naked, feed the poor - it was a breeze - wasn't it?

Loading the car with pickle jars - enough for a restaurant, tuna fish, soup, bread, candy and clothes - and did we have clothes! The trunk of Fanny's late model car was stuffed to the max with everything we had. We had to push at the trunk to shut it. Finally, we were on our way, the four of us, God's best, doing what He had ordered us to do and getting rapid heart beats the closer we came. We got to the outskirts, drove past all those filled cabbage fields, but no one was out today. After all, it was late afternoon on a Sunday. No one worked on Sunday, especially just to pick a cabbage. As we drove the main road, everything looked so beautiful and green, the weather was cool, but the sun was still out for a couple more hours before it would start its descent. It was quiet out here, peaceful. We passed small shacks on the way - some abandoned over time, but still standing. Then we passed a small brick building on the right. It was built next to a drainage ditch. It had been painted green many years ago, but now it just peeled and showed the rust stains and cracks the paint was meant to hide. There were six or seven doors on it. Some had screen doors, but the doors didn't keep much out. They hung crooked so big spaces of light shone through some with cracks down the middle of the door panels letting the weather in. The screen doors had none or little screening left to them and just hung usually on one hinge not even able to close.

Surely, no one could be here! There goes that naive attitude, so we went on. We turned down a dirt road and drove over bumps for about a mile. We came to a small building and stopped to look. It was a dog kennel where the farmers kept their hunting dogs. It held about ten dogs and every steel cubical shined like glass. The papers on the bottom must have just been changed. It didn't even smell like you would have expected it to. Next to it was a separate small shed which held their food, enough food I guess to feed them for a year - it was unbelievable. But not a worker, still! So back we went over the bumps once again.

This time a car was coming up towards us, so we figured we would stop him. We did and he got out of his car. It was a black man who obviously hadn't shaved that day or had time to pick out his hair or shower for that matter. He was well overweight and his shirt was a medium, he needed an x-large. As he talked, he never took his unlit stogy out of his mouth, which looked as though he'd been chewing on all day. We asked him if he knew where the migrants were and if he knew a man named Noah. That was the only name we had to go on. With a stogy dangling from his mouth and trying to stand up straight and pulling in his basketball stomach so he could possibly pull up his pants to meet his shirt, he stared a while then asked us "Why, whos wantin' ta know?" We told him of our intentions. It seemed fine with him. He told us to follow him. So off we went, again.

Strangely enough, he took us up back to the old green building. What for? No one could possibly be in this awful place. As we drove up over this little make-shift bridge that crossed over the drainage ditch, we stopped in front. He got out of his old car, which in its day in New York City would have been called a "pimpmobile," with its faded out dice and about six or seven other things hanging from the front mirror. They all shook as his weight lifted from the car. He yelled out as he stood there. "Hey, you all come out here now, there's some good peoples here who wanta give ya all somethin'." Just like when Glenda the good witch called the munchkins out of hiding in the Wizard of Oz, so did these people. They came out one by one shy as little puppies not knowing if they've done good or bad.

They were a mixture of ages, some looked like they should be home with their parents still having Sunday dinner - so why weren't they? Some were in their sixties and seventies, so why weren't they living a good retired life somewhere just cashing their social security checks once a month? My husband jumped in quickly to take charge, thank God! I mean we couldn't just stand there looking at this group. Let's do what we came here for and go home. This way we would now have a good Thanksgiving, guilt fee because we now were helping the less fortunate. We gave out the food we had, a little to each person. Then I thought, where did that big pickle jar go? We each figured one of the others gave it out to someone, and let it be.

Then we opened the trunk, and obviously we had too many clothes for this group, but we gave out what we could and tried to fit each person. Strangely enough, they really didn't care if they got mens or ladies clothes. They took anything as long as it was going to keep them warm. Everything was given out and the trunk was stilled filled with clothes.

We asked them all if after they put their stuff away if they would like to pray with us. We weren't sure if maybe they would disappear behind those cracked and weathered doors, but amazingly enough, one by one they all came back out. We all stood in a circle. Some had already had their new jackets on. Others had the socks and shoes on. What a feeling it gave us to see this. So then we stood in front of this old green building on this cold damp rocky dirt that was beginning to freeze my feet even through my warm socks and sneakers. Holding hands together with the people from the fields, I had a lady on my left who maybe weighed all of 95 pounds. She wore old polyester pants that I'm sure had been worn and slept in hundreds of times, here matted hair tied up in an old dirty bandanna. Her face was worn and so wrinkled you could see cuts in it where it was so dry it just cracked. Still, you could see a sparkle in here eye as she smiled at me with her high boney cheeks. She nodded at me almost in a bowing gesture and just simply said "ma'am." This made me very uncomfortable and confused; after all, I was just turning thirty in December and she had to be at least in her late sixties or early seventies. I was brought up to respect my elders and to treat them with honor so to speak, no matter who they were. The man on my right reached out and took my hand. I had to actually look down to see if he had gloves on because his hand was so hard. All I could think of was it felt like very heavy leather, but it wasn't covered with anything - it was his hand. Again, like the lady he smiled, nodded and simply said "Sister."

Alan led us all in prayer. It was wonderful as we stood there. You could feel the smile of the Lord over this circle. Suddenly, it didn't matter who was who, where we were, or that my feet were cold. We all stood for the same reason, to thank God and to give Him glory for all that He supplied on this day. Alan went on and with my eyes closed, I could hear these fifteen other voices humming in agreement and saying things like "you got that right," "yes sir - preach it brother," "you tell 'em," and a lot of just "ah - ah." The women sometimes sang the old Negro spirituals. As I stood amidst all of this, I felt so happy and sad all at the same time, but I also thought, now this is church! Suddenly, I wanted to tell everyone about this wonderful happening. I wanted them all to experience this and most of all, wanted to come back!

The circle broke, and we started to say our goodbyes. They were thanking us for everything. Then the little lady from my left stepped forward and told us here name. It was Bernice. She asked us to pray for her friend and we said of course we would. Then in her meekness she asked us what we were doing to do with all the leftover clothes. We really didn't have an answer. Her next statement shocked us. She asked if we would consider taking then down to the next camp. She said they were in need also. WHAT NEXT CAMP!?

Now the man we followed to this camp had already lowered himself back into his car. I asked Bernice what his name was and who he was, and she told me "He Mr. Noah, he the boss man." So this was Noah. Why was he so defensive of his identity when we first met him? I caught him before he was backing out. I leaned into his opened window to ask him about the camp down the street and as I did, I saw the large jar of pickles peeking out from one of our coats on the floor of his back seat. Why was he hiding them? Did he need them? Why would he need them? He's the boss man. I ignored what I saw. I went right on to ask him about the other camp and how we could get there from where we were. We didn't want to end up lost again. So he told us and even agreed to take us there. So off we went again with Mr. Noah in the lead.

This was a little bigger place, but it still had that weather - beaten and aged look about it. This one had some windows on it and some still had glass in them, some had only boards. It all looked like it was going to be the same scenario as the first labor camp (as they were called). Later, we named the first camp "Bernice's." As we pulled into this camp, we got out of the car and immediately opened the trunk. There was only two or three guys outside walking around and two sitting over in an old yellow bus that they used to transport the workers to and from the fields. One of the men asked us what we were doing there, so Mr. Noah stepped right in and told them. Well when they heard free clothes and food, they took off inside to tell the others. Within seconds we had about thirty five to forty five men, women and children swarmed all around us. It was an overwhelming feeling. We had no control, and we were certainly outnumbered. Some of these people were very rude poking and pushing trying to pull clothes out of the car. Others just stood back and waited and watched. I looked at faces as I stood there. The faces were about the same as the ones at "Bernice's Camp." They looked very hard. Their skin looked like black leather that had been dried out in the sun. Some of them, their hands were so bad that they had deep cuts in their palms, but they didn't bleed because the callouses that covered them were so thick nothing could penetrate. Some only had slippers on, and a couple of men had only the soles of shoes on their feet with string to tie them on. Some were bare footed with rags tied to their feet to cover sores. One lady came out to see what was going on. I saw here standing in the background with her two kids - one two years old and the other three months, two boys. Her name was Orlene. The two-year old stood clutching his mother's leg. He was shoeless and wore only pajamas that I knew were never washed and were at least two sizes too small. The baby wore only a diaper. The smell of alcohol was everywhere mixed with body odor and a musty dirt smell. As I stood there, I knew I definitely wasn't in "Oz" - actually I didn't feel like I was in Florida anymore. Scenes like this weren't suppose to be in the good and great "US of A" - what was going on? Maybe I was really a missionary in Haiti or just maybe this was really happening. This was the way it is for all these people. This was their reality!

Having a weakness for babies, I made my way over to the lady with the two little boys. I said "hi" to her and told her my name as I played with the baby. She just looked at me for a long time, almost like she was afraid of me and shouldn't take her eyes off me. I figured I should tell her who we were and why we were there. As I started, I hear Alan very loudly say he wanted everyone's attention and to back off. Then he took control. He explained that we had no idea all these people were out here and that we didn't have enough food and clothes for everyone, but were gonna be praying and that God would supply. So was Alan feeling the same as I? I mean none of us even spoke on the way over to this camp. We just sat in shock after "Bernice's," but I guess God made it clear to all of us, we were coming back! Before we left, we told everyone to tell us if there was anything that they really needed and during the week, we would try to get it for them. Again before leaving this camp, we made a big circle and prayed with everyone, and we especially prayed for the material things they had requested. Now it was really hard to understand how we could have even thought that we could have come out here, see what we did and not return or try to help. Although many people have done just that. With a lot of people, the attitude is that "these people have been doing this for hundreds of years, so it's not going to kill them now." That's one comment I have really learned to hate and resent. It always make me think where were these people during their history classes when they learned about the Civil War and the free South? Where were they when

John F. Kennedy fought so hard to fight against discrimination and racism in this country? I can't understand how some of these people can just watch TV commercials for "feed the children," or scenes from Ethiopia or one that shows the dirt and disgust of Haiti. Well, they need to see the dirt and disgust and outright injustice that sits right outside of their own little "Oz," in our great country of America! A place where with all its wealth and education, this should never happen!

Well, we did the only thing that we knew we could do after seeing what we did on this day. We made a commitment to be back to help. Little did we know, all the things we would witness after that day. We could have never imagined!

CHAPTER THREE

Camp Education

Our commitment is now eight years old. A lot of things have happened in that time, some good, and some very, very sad. We have seen a lot of workers come and go. Some go into better situations, although they couldn't get much worse than what they were in.

After the first couple of weeks of going to "Bernice's Camp" and "Sammy's Camp" (that was the second camp), we found out about three more. So we were now visiting about 175 to 200 people every Saturday or Sunday. As time went on, and it didn't take much time at all, maybe a month, we started to become friends. It got so we looked forward to seeing our friends on the weekends.

I got friendly with Orlene and her two boys. One windy and blustery Sunday when we went out, she invited me into her room "where she stay at." We never walked into the building at "Sammy's Camp" - we really never had to - as soon as the workers saw our cars drive up, they came out in a wave. Well, this day I went in. There was a small hallway, on either side of the hallway there were doorways, some had doors some had dirty old cloth material hanging across the openings, some nothing. The light that snuck in through the doorways showed all the thick dust that hung in the musty damp air. The floors were cement as were the walls. Someone asked me to describe it once, and all I could think of was to go and stand in your stocking feet about 11:00 PM in mid January in your garage. That's what it is like to live in one of these rooms in the migrant camps or labor camps, as they were also called.

As I got to Orlene's room, I just stood in the doorway. I didn't really know what to do. The stench was so strong and bad. I thought I'd be sick, but the sight I was beholding made me want to cry. The feelings I had were very confusing. Here I stood feeling sad and almost angry at all this and yet she was so proud to show me her place, her home, her world! All that was everything to her, was nothing more than the 8x10 cement cubical with no windows, but she was one of this lucky ones, she did have a door. I learned that she did have a husband, and his name was Gerald. I even saw him, although I didn't really get to meet him. He was laying stone cold drunk on their twin size mattress that lay on the damp cement floor.

At night, this same mattress held him and Orlene and their two small boys. They had one pillow that was not covered except for the old stains of blood and dirt. The blankets looked like a pile of rags heaped on the mattress. The whole time I stood there Gerald never moved. I found out later his drunkenness was his pay for working overtime - a kind of reward instead of money, of course! In the corner of the room was an old make-up mirror and table; which in its day was probably beautiful, but now the mirror was all cracked, the table had a drawer missing and one of the broken legs made it wobble. On it sat an opened jar of mayonnaise, some sardines and other culinary wonders that weren't even recognizable, and I'm sure were not edible. I asked her where the baby slept, and she pointed to the mattress on the floor. Just the thought of it made me shutter inside. I did all that I could do not to cry.

I made the excuse we would wake Gerald up if we stayed and talked any longer, so we walked back outside, but not before walking through the building. Truly the scenic route! I got to meet Orlene's sister Elsie, her husband Slim and their two children. They were different and you could see it right off. Elsie had her hair in curlers and one thing I noticed she didn't have that stale smell of alcohol on her. Her clothes were by no means new or stylish, but they were fairly clean. Her children wore shoes on their feet. They probably would fit them better in about a year or so, but at least their feet were covered. That's the way Elsie looked at it and she was right. Her husband Slim was a real worker. He was about 6'9" tall and strong as a bull. His hands were the first thing I noticed. They were as big as a baseball glove, and just as tough. When I met him, he was working on an old beat-up car that someone had dumped. He told me he was going to fix it, so he could take his family off the camp when he wanted and go fishing or go to town. You could see in his eyes he wanted out and wanted a better life for his wife and children, and he was going to get it! He hadn't lost that hope yet! Even their room was different. They didn't have much of anything, but what they did have was there in their room, and you could see Elsie liked things in order, unlike her sister. Their room was bigger than the rest. They got it when one of the crew chiefs' sons moved out. It had a door and a window, so it was a little brighter, it measured about 10' x 12". Elsie and Slim had a double mattress, but it was set up on blocks with wood. The boys slept on an old couch, one at one end, the other at the other end. She had a hot plate and an electric fry pan set on a little table. Slim got them when someone threw them out. I guess that makes true the old saying "one man's junk is another man's treasure."

Next to Slim and Elsie's room was what everyone called the "Bull Pen." It was a room where all the single and mostly new guys stayed. It was one of the rooms that had no door - only a piece of cloth hanging in the doorway. I pulled it back to see what was in the room. It was terrible - nothing more than a storage room to keep this crew chief from feeling guilty. At least he could say he had these guys off the street with a roof over their heads, but that was about all he could say. This room had no heat. It was lined with old cots and mattresses that were so bad they used newspaper to stuff into holes hoping to keep some of the firmness in them. All it did was give a place for the roaches and spiders that held this place hostage a place to hide and multiply. About twenty men filled this dark, damp cave. All the men were black Americans except two that were Spanish.

People are always under the assumption that migrant workers are from different countries, wetbacks or illegals. In some cases, it's true especially in states like California or Texas. We also have them in Florida. But on the whole, our migrants are American born and raised. Some are World War II and Vietnam veterans. This is all they know. It is a way of life for them and there is nothing wrong with it if it's by choice and it is being run by Florida State Laws for migrant workers. As we quickly learned, this was not the case in at least four out of five camps we visited. These camps are owned by the farmers who must be blind in one eye and unable to see out of the other. The workers in these camps are owned by the crew chief, straw bosses, or boss men. I'll explain why I say owned. Now we all know that slavery was abolished over one hundred years ago, but let me tell you how this little system works and let you decide on whether slavery still exists in this United States of ours!

CHAPTER FOUR

The Lie

A man goes out with a van or big yellow bus, you know the kind we all hated to ride when we were in school. He drives through some inner-city "housing projects" all over the States of Florida, North Carolina and Georgia, usually preying on street people or low income people. These people usually get approached while they're standing on the street or just hanging around in a group. The person in charge will approach them and go on to tell them he's looking for workers. He'll tell them they will get room and board free and transportation to "sunny" Florida. Some have been told they would be living in hotel-like surroundings, with everything they need, including good pay, steady work. What more could you ask for? It sound real good, especially when you have a family and you've been out of work for a good long while, with nothing in sight except more hanging around and more welfare. So, they except this better than life offer. In most cases, they have to be ready to leave in 24 hours, so they get their stuff together which usually isn't much. Some men get on the bus with nothing more than the clothes on their backs and maybe all of

$5 in their pockets. The driver tells them "don't worry, we'll get you some clothes, good food, a nice bed and plenty to drink."

Well, the trip eventually comes to an end and reality usually settles in after the first night of sleeping on an old damp mattress used by about 200 other people before them. Quickly, now they realize they've been cheated, lied to, scammed. Now they're away from home, away from who they know and what they know, in the middle of this "cabbage sea," miles from "no where." So you might say why not leave, hitch a ride, get out. Here's one reason - the clincher - the sting! The bus driver conveniently failed to tell these men one little detail. The detail of a small fee for the ride to "Utopia," in some cases $85. Since they have no money and naturally haven't worked yet, they automatically go into debt to the crew chief for $85. Of course, there may be work that first couple of weeks, but the likelihood of that is next to none! The men do have to eat whether they work or not, so the crew chief is of course, obliging to this need and, it is a law, these men must get fed. After all, they were promised "good food." So food they will get, usually two meals, but there are times they get three. The dinner meal which is the best meal of the deal is usually something like a couple of scoops of rice and a piece of pork fat on top or a piece of kielbasa. I also have seen them receive a bologna sandwich (two pieces of bread and a slice of bologna) or a piece of bread and a scoop of hash. Now this is a meal given to a grown man after working from sunup to sundown in the fields; some times in rain and cold or 100 degree weather. What a deal you get; all this for a mere $45 a week whether you work or not. So have you been keeping track? If you're not working you are now in debt that first week for $130 - SO FAR!

Every boss likes to keep his workers happy and the crew chiefs are no exception especially when the men aren't working. So to keep everyone happy and to keep things light around the camp, why not serve up some wine. Better still, some 150 proof wine - better known as MD or Mad Dog. Usually it costs at the small grocers in town at Lumbell about $1.99 a fifth, but don't forget you've got delivery charges now so this same bottle cost $6. On a weekend, an average worker can go through maybe 5 or 6 of these bottles, but no problem - just put it on the tab, that's another $36. Now this man or women is looking at $166 and he hasn't included the water and electric bill that gets divided up between everyone, even the children. So that means couples like Slim and Elsie, who are trying to keep their family together at the camp, have to pay their two children's fair share of this bill. The children also have to pay to eat from the kitchen so most of the workers with children just share what they get with their children at mealtimes.

One special weekend, we arrived and everyone was outside. There was a big metal drum in the middle of the crowd with a big fire coming out of it. They were cooking and let me tell you it smelled great! We asked what was going on and they said "The boss man he bring us fish today, and we gettin' em' ready to be eaten." Naturally, it was assumed by us that everyone was going to be eating that day, and pretty good at that. So we decided to put most of the can goods away and go on to the next camp. Everyone was so involved in watching this fish cook we figured we'd just slip away. Not that easy! We started to get back into our van and car when Orlene came running out with her baby in her arms. She was yelling "Wer you all goin' now? I aint seen you yeat." So we stopped! We explained that since such a good meal was being served that we were leaving. Her face just dropped, and she just stood there like we had scolded her and were walking out on her. We asked her what was wrong. She went on to explain about this great feast that was about to be served up. Sure the boss man had indeed caught all this fish and was even cooking it for the workers, BUT, and that's a pretty big word, not all the workers.

He had picked the chosen who he wanted to share this good food with. When he arrived, he called out for all the workers to come out so he could show them just what he had. He had them empty out his truck of the buckets of fish and light the barrel of fire to cook it all. He had the women and some men gut and clean all the fish. Then as they watched and waited, he went down the line of workers like a true overseer, and a man of power, making sure all the workers understood this power he had. Making his way down the line, he took his time and pointed to each one who would eat and telling those to leave who would not be eating that day. As he said yes to the "chosen few" they smiled at him and said "thankya sir, thankya very much." It came time for Ms. Orlene and her family. She stood there with her baby and little boy, and he told her "NO", maybe next time you can show me better work, and with that she walked away with her kids. We took all the others that didn't get fed that day and gave then can goods and made sure we picked out can goods that would give them a little more substance than usual.

This feast that happened that day isn't something that happens all that often. Most of the time, the workers eat off the kitchen like it was explained. You may say once the people get working they'll just pay off all that they got into debt with. Sounds easy enough. It's a shame it just doesn't happen that way. Unless in one case in about 200 that person could not drink or smoke or eat off the kitchen. Also the ride into town for whatever need, would cost them in most cases $10. The whole thing is just their way of putting people in a hamster's cage and letting them run in the wheel, go round and round, get tired, and go absolutely nowhere.

As time goes on, we learned how wrong this system is, not only being illegal but humanly unjust. Just like slavery!

CHAPTER FIVE

Jose'

Miguel and Jose are two Spanish men at "Sammy's Camp." When they first arrived, they were very quiet and kept to themselves. Miguel took care of Jose although he was much younger then him. Jose could not speak English at all. When we all first met, Fanny and Ed took them both under their wings since they spoke Spanish as their first language. Jose was thrilled to meet them.

Miguel was maybe 5'6" tall and a very small framed man. He came from Puerto Rico, didn't drink or smoke and hadn't been in trouble. Something that is very rare in the labor camps. His plan was to work and send his pay to his family in Puerto Rico so they could survive and maybe have a little better life. He had a lot of hope, you could see it in his face. Even the reality of where he was now living wasn't going to get him down. He had a plan and was going to try to stick to it - they key word here, TRY!

Jose was a thin man. He was from Puerto Rico also. He met up with Miguel in route to this labor camp. He unlike Miguel had no real family. So for Jose working was strictly survival, for himself. Working the camps had become a way of life for him, and you could see he had become accustom to it. He didn't have too many questions, no expectations for life - just to survive. Jose was very quiet and all his years of drinking had left him a bit shaky on his feet so at times he would walk like he was unsure of each step he was about to take. He always made it out to see us and always with his arm out stretched waiting for that warm handshake or hug. Miguel always would interpret for us if Fanny and Ed weren't here, with their fluent Spanish. Even when no one was around, his almost toothless smile and very easy flowing hand gesture seemed enough to put his point across to communicate! He mostly kept with Miguel and that kept the two of them out of trouble. On weekends, when everyone was drinking hard, it seemed no one could stay out of anyone else's way - then trouble!

This is how it happened with Jose and Samuel (another worker). The weather had gotten cold very quickly, almost overnight. That particular Saturday, we decided not to go out to the camps because Alan felt we didn't have enough clothes or food to give out to everyone. It is very hard to go out to the camps when things are low especially if the weather is cold or they haven't been working steadily - they need so much. One thing we didn't know, another church group was going out that day. They had boxes of clothes and some food with them to give out. It was great that they went, but not knowing the people out at the camps, they were a little timid. When they arrived, they took the boxes of things they had, and set them out on the ground for everyone to help themselves. This caused complete chaos - everything from the boxes went flying, people were grabbing and pulling like it was a bargain basement sale at the mall. Somewhere in that box was a very nice warm man's jacket.

As Jose reached in his long veined fingers, he found it and pulled it out. He then realized Samuel had a hold of it also. So the survival struggle began. They pulled back and forth both tugging at the old brown jacket as if the lining contained gold. They yelled and cursed at each other for several minutes, until Samuel slammed his half down, leaving Jose standing there holding the jacket. At the moment, Jose felt like the victor. He had won the jacket, and he sent Samuel, a much younger and stronger man, in retreat. Or had he? That moment faded fast for Jose as Samuel reappeared outside holding in his hand a machete, the same one he used to cut the cabbage. Jose froze where he stood. Samuel ran towards Jose like a possessed animal yelling and cursing. He rammed Jose knocking him in the chest causing his frail body to slam on the cold dirt ground. Jose never had a chance to recover or even attempt to get himself up. Samuel then jumped onto him stabbing Jose in the chest. Everyone stood watching, some yelling for Samuel to stop but to no avail. It was over in seconds. Samuel stood up over Jose's body, watching the life pour out of him, then turned and ran towards the wooded area at the end of the cabbage field.

While all the other workers and the children stood watching such a horrifying murder, they knew all to well in their hearts they would never repeat to authorities the truth of what they had just witnessed. The fear they had in becoming a witness against someone else in the camp they lived with was greater than anything they could stand. Also the fear of just tying themselves with an authoritative figure, what would the boss man say? All this fear paralyzed them from helping to get Samuel convicted of this brutal crime. The people from the church that were there said they never actually saw the event take place so they couldn't be of any real help. The police came and they did arrest Samuel, he said of course it was self defense. He said he feared for his life up against Jose. The ambulance came and took Jose to the hospital. They brought him into surgery, but it was too late. Hours later, Alan and I got a phone call from someone in the Sheriffs Department, who knew we did work with the migrants, telling us Jose had died. They asked if we knew of any family members he may have had, but we knew of none. He was buried that week in an unmarked grave in the pauper field, with the rest of the so-called insignificant people. Forgotten! Never by us and certainly not by God. You see, Jose had asked the Lord into his life one week earlier to his death.

Samuel was a good strong worker "The man" needed him, so he was bailed out of jail the next day. He got probation and an order not to drink while on probation. The irony of the whole thing was Samuel never even took the jacket, but Jose died over a simple thing like keeping warm.

Along with everything else, the labor camps have their own laws but not much order. They have become little worlds of their own that no one wants to bother with; not the police, not even the farmers who own the land they live on.

For instance, another fight occurred one night. One of the workers got pushed into a fire that was built to keep warm by. His whole right arm and shoulder and a part of his chest was burned leaving his tough black skin melted off to where the pink raw skin showed. We had arrived at the camp about two days after this had happened. He had his arm wrapped in dirty rags. Two of our friends that were helping us at the time, Carlos and Maurice, took it upon themselves to take him to the hospital. If they hadn't, he would have just been expected to go on working like he had been with his arm open to infection, possibly killing him.

Another instance with Jose, before his death was he had gotten very sick. A lot of the older people at the camps were sick. The weather had been very cold and rainy and a freeze was coming so the field had to be picked in order to save the plants no matter the cost to the workers and putting aside their health. The crew chief came into the camp this particular night about 10:00 PM. He made a sweep inside the building yelling and banging on doors for everyone to get up and out. It was time for work - NOW! He wanted everyone NO exceptions, not even for Jose. His body ached from head to toe, he laid their shivering cold even though to the touch his body felt like it was burning up, and he could hardly take a breath without coughing near to passing out. With all of that he went out to the fields to work. Midday the following day we saw him, laying on his cot soaking wet. He had gotten up to take a shower thinking he would feel better, not thinking he had no towel to dry himself off, He had only his clothes to use. So that night about 10:30 PM, Alan couldn't stand the thought of how Jose looked when he saw him earlier. Alan called Ed and within 20 minutes, they were out the door with blankets, a portable heater, some clothes, aspirin and cough medicine. Jose did make it through. Although Jose was just one worker out of many, there were many other workers who have been in this position too many times to count.

There was another man in the same camp who had broken his leg, after a fall off a tractor. The crew chief set his leg and his man was told to work, it would be fine. Not even in the outskirts of "Oz" were people treated in this manner. You hear of things like this happening in South Africa and our country leaders are furious over it. The United Nations start to yell "Human Rights Act." What about here, what about these people, our own people, God's people. Sometimes, I wonder how we, as Americans, expect to hold respect from other countries when we can't even take care of our own people at home. This issue with migrant camps shouldn't be all that difficult. After all, it's something I found. It's happening in plain sight right in people's backyard. There are inspectors who get paid to inspect migrant camps. Crew chiefs have to file special papers when running a labor camp and traveling from state to state. If all this is happening, then this means people are out there supposedly being paid, so there should be ledger books being kept and taxes being paid, but are they? Why is it when all these accidents occur, no one is ever allowed to collect workmen's compensation? Or why isn't when they reach a certain age they collect social security? I found most of these workers do not even have social security numbers or if they did, they have since lost them. I know because I got a lot of the workers their numbers again and birth certificates. All this take a little work, of course, but people are getting paid to take care of all of this, so why isn't it done?

CHAPTER SIX

Paraguay Migrants

There are some wonderful people in South Florida; one who is a lawyer, one who is a Harvard Law School graduate. They have dedicated their time and talents to helping the migrant workers and making sure their rights are not violated. They can't help them all, but they try.

One year I got a phone call from one of these "saints." She explained how she got my phone number and went on to tell me who she was and what their organization does. It was great help; at last someone that knew the ropes, and most importantly someone who knew the laws and how to enforce them. She also explained in a nice way, although she may call now and again, we should never meet. When I asked her why, she told me it wouldn't be good for us to be connected with their group in case of court cases should come up. This way, if we were not involved, our relationship with the crew chiefs and farmers would always remain the same. They wouldn't try to keep us away.

The first camp they went to was what we called "Eddie's Camp." It was a camp of mostly men except for the co-ed and the couple of men who thought they were women. At this camp, we had about five Spanish speaking men, four who knew no English at all. The one man knew only very little English. These men were from Paraguay. They were here on work visas and their only goal was to send as much money home as possible. When the law group went to check out the camp, they asked a lot of questions trying to feel things out and give them handouts which told them of their rights as a migrant worker in Florida. The workers themselves didn't say much - they got shy about who to trust and who not to trust. The law group understood this, because they have been through this so many times before. They knew they needed a few more visits before they could win confidences. As they expected on the visit to the camp the workers started to talk with them and finally even started to answer some of the questions, and it didn't take long for them to learn they did have rights. Also they learned that those rights had been violated and in some cases taken away all together. The following week was different. This time when the law group came out, the Spanish men were waiting for them. They told them they wanted to talk. One of the woman for the law group, Beverly, spoke fluent Spanish which made it all the more comfortable for them to tell her their story.

They began to tell her about how they got there, why they came in the first place. But the shocker was, what's been happening since they got there. It seems the crew chief took their visas and their green cards that prove they were in the United States legally. When he took them, he told them now he owned them. After hearing this, I understood why when we went out to the camp, they looked so defeated. They usually would be together just squatted down on the ground just talking or just picking at the grass while they stared out at nothing with empty eyes. As soon as Beverly got all the story down on paper, she, of course, told them not to worry, all would be taken care of.

Everything moved fast from then on. The next day, the head attorney for the organization went right to the crew chief and gave him twenty four hours to give the five Spanish men their green cards back. His alternative was to have the FBI on his doorstep and to be charged with kidnaping and holding persons against their will. Mr. Boss Man as cool as he could be just said "Ah! You could have 'em. They ain't worth notin', no how anyway." He did return the green cards the next day, but as we and the legal group knew, these Spanish men could have never stayed at this camp any longer. The boss man would make sure it would be nothing more than a living hell for them. He would have worked them to death.

It was about 3:00 AM when the station wagon pulled into the camp with its lights out. The five Spanish men were huddled in one room waiting. The legal group knew this had to happen this way. Everyone knew the crew chief Mr. Alex would be at his canal front home with his Lincoln Continental in front and brand new truck parked out front, in "Oz." Also about 99 percent of the workers at this time would be passed out from their rewards of whiskey for working that day. They hurried into the car each with a small bag of belongings each, and they were on their way. They were taken to a Christian run camp in South Florida.

The legal people helped in many instances for the next year. They helped straighten out things that were going on for quite some time. One of the biggest ways was in getting three of the labor camps completely shut down which in Lumbell took a lot of doing. It was a way of life coming to a close, it showed change, and people there weren't used to strangers changing things.

These particular camps were closed for things like selling crack cocaine, selling of alcohol and tobacco, poor living conditions, all to say the least. You see, all labor camps depending on the size, can only hold an "x" amount of people, need to have so many bathroom facilities for "x" amount of people, and at least two meals a day. Now let's just take these three for instance. The camp we called "Sammy's" was greatly overcrowded especially just before picking season because he'd need so much help. So even if he should only house thirty people, he would have fifty or sixty workers living there. To squeeze everyone in, men and women had to share rooms whether they agreed or not! This camp had two bathrooms outside the building, each had a shower in them that I wouldn't wash a dog in. It was a hot shower as long as you happened to be the first to use it and took a five minute shower. One of the toilets didn't have a seat on it so it basically was a hole in the ground. Also these so-called bathrooms were pretty far from where the workers slept. This was a problem for all the camps, especially during the cold weather. This may seen like a small problem, but what it caused was the workers bringing these white buckets that were left around the camp from seed or paint into their rooms and use them for a toilet - not very sanitary. I don't care where you live!

Especially not sanitary when you think the next morning they would take it and dump it into the fields. They would then go out to the fields to work all day and without any portable toilets out there, (like the law requires, but also costs money) - so you have more unsanitary conditions. The workers would have to relieve themselves during the day and they would have to do this in the fields were they worked. This was another fight the legal people had on their hands. Something like this situation goes far beyond just laws. It's peoples' dignity. You're stripping them of their self worth - it just isn't human! The same old story exist "it's been like this for hundreds of years, so it's okay."

Another big problem for the labor camps is health care. Who should be responsible for this? How do they get to clinics to be seen by nurses and doctors. Do the crew chiefs have a right to tell them they cannot go? For the past eight years, we have seen a lot of problems such as high blood pressure, TB, cancer, skin problems of all kinds, diabetes and a wide-spread of venereal diseases go untreated because no one cared. The attitude usually being if your not dead, you work!

We met one worker at "Bernice's Camp" that was so ridden with syphilis he was blind in one eye and had lost most of the sight out of the other. He was losing his hair because the disease had caused his skin to get so badly rashed. He walked with a cane because he was partly paralyzed. And with all of this, he dragged his decaying 30 year old body to work, to keep this roof over his head.

This was an all-to-common situation at the labor camps.

CHAPTER SEVEN

Eunice

Her name was Eunice, and she was my friend, a mom, a wife, and a labor camp worker. When I first met her, she had three children, like me. Her youngest, a girl not a year old yet, like mine, and also named Nicole, like mine. As time went on, she had two more children, boys and so did I. So we had a lot in common. Every time we were out at the camp, the two of us had a lot to talk about. We were the same age, but here I sat in "Oz" and still very healthy.

On Eunice's fourth pregnancy, she noted she had a lump in her stomach. Her pregnancy went fine. She had a healthy baby boy. The lump remained and she bled on and off from it for months. The doctors did nothing for her. She was kept in the hospital for a couple of days, but then sent home. They said there was nothing they could do for her. It would be very costly. Even with all of this, she still worked as much as she could and also managed to get pregnant again. And again, she had a fine healthy baby boy, but this time, it wasn't an easy delivery. It left her tired and frail, the lump in her stomach turned out to be a malignant tumor. Caring for her children at times was impossible. The only medication they would give her cost $50 per bottle for one and $45 per bottle for the other. Also she was expected to pay for these medicines herself. Being a migrant, she had no real address to speak of and that is a requirement of welfare. Needles to say, she went without any medication many, many times. There were times when she would in all her pain, drive her old beat-up car to a little country store near the camp and call our home for help. When I would pick up the phone I could hardly make out the weak voice on the other end.

One particular time I remember, we went to meet her at the drugstore to help pay for the medicine. When we got there, she was rolling all over the seat in the car, trying not to scream. The pain was so bad her eyes would roll up in her head and all she could do was hope the pain would knock her out. You see, even when she would be this bad, she was unable to be hospitalized, she had no medical insurance to cover her illness. And the doctors said there wasn't anything they could do for her anyway. God is good though. Another crew chief, a woman, who had her camp up the road, took her in and all her children. This crew chief was one of the rare good ones. She ran a good camp and tried very hard to do it by the book. Once she was living with Mary, the boss woman, hospice, a wonderful organization who cares for terminally ill patients, started visits to Eunice. They did everything to make her as comfortable as they could. She was brought a hospital bed and all her medication and nurses that came everyday to visit. This went on for almost a year and during this time, she was bedridden and had lost the little weight she had. I was told later by another woman at another camp when her day finally came and she past away in peace and was happy. When they came in her small room and found she had past, they say she just lay their like she was asleep with her bible in her arms.

Eunice was a good person and she was strong. I believe to this day, caring and loving her children the way she did kept her going. She had hope for them and she made sure they were going to be cared for after she was gone, and they were. The woman Mary kept them as her own making sure they were always clean and dressed nice, and in school. The older boys were a hand full, but one went on into the army. The other had trouble with the law and was put in jail. Although before his time, he was freed from jail and is now a preacher in Northern Florida. Her oldest daughter has a child of her own, and had joined the job corp and got an education and job and still lives in Florida. The younger children are in school and all doing well. None work on the farms. So Eunice's dream for a future will live on in her children. The tragedy is the way the so-called "system" allowed this person, this somebody, this woman that should have mattered suffer relentlessly and beg for help while people around her pretended not to see her pain.

CHAPTER EIGHT

"My Cover"

As I said earlier, the labor camps are their own little worlds with their own laws. Up the dirt road, a bit from where Eunice use to stay was another amp. We called it "Eddie's." There were all men at this camp except the cook and another girl. We called it Eddies because he happened to be the first person we met. Eddie was the biggest, the loudest, the strongest and the drunkest of all the workers. His father was the crew chief here, you remember him - Mr. Noah! Well, Eddie was a real chip off the old block. The first time we met him, I almost choked from the smell of stale booze on him as he walked towards us still drunk from the night before. He had no shoes on, but his feet were so thick and heavy he could have walked on glass and have never known it. His shirt was only buttoned with two buttons so his big black belly hung over his half zipped pants. When he got close enough, he stopped with his feet apart and his huge arms that could barely cross over his chest and yelled "what you all want?" And with that shout, it sent him rocking from side to side. "You betta be gettin' outta here or we'll be havin' trouble." Well, believe me when I tell you, I was ready to go. Eddie was the kind of guy everyone listed to and agreed with, while he was around. So we told him as we had at the other camps. Eddie said it was okay for us to stay - but he never took his eyes off us. We would have to earn his trust. He saw us giving out the food and clothes, nothing much interested him. He did have one request though. He told us next time we came out he wanted "Red Man." We had no idea what Red Man was, but we figured no problem. Who was going to argue with him? I think he could see we didn't know what it was, so he told us, it was "chew", chewing tobacco. As he explained, what he had left of it ran out the corner of his mouth, leaving a brown stream over his two day old beard. Every so often he would spit it out and we'd try real hard not to gag!

Eddie was something else, a real character. No one crossed him and when they did, you would see the payment for it on their faces - in the form of black swollen eyes, cut lips, swollen cheeks, a broken arm. No one would have pity on the man or woman who was stupid enough to cross this man. He was strong and tough, but he couldn't read or write and behind his back, the other men would say, "what a half wit" he was or call him "the crazy man." Later on, we found out he was the product of incest. Eddie liked to drink. He was very seldom sober. He would walk a few miles down the road to a bar room. He wasn't welcome there. It was only for the "white boys" mostly the farmers' sons hung out there after work. His money on the other hand was very much welcome, but only through the back door of this "classy" establishment. Sometimes, when work was going pretty steady, they would make deliveries out to the camp for the convenience of the workers. They would bring out a few cases of beer and the old favorite MD and of course, some cartons of cigarettes. They would set up in the kitchen and sell everything at double the cost. Of course, if one of the workers didn't have the money, they would charge it for them, and all of this without Visa or Master Charge! I'm sure the Tobacco and Liquor Licensing Board would have loved to have seen this. The same system that failed Eunice continues to turn their backs. When this special service would happen, it would put all the workers way behind in their debts. The crew chief usually would make sure all the tobacco and alcohol was gone for that night. The workers were drunk and happy and he was a man with money.

I remember one very special time that really surprised me when it came to knowing Eddie. I was about eight and one half months pregnant with my fourth child and we had gone out to the camps. I was saying goodbye for a while because I would be having the baby soon and going out on all those bumpy roads really wasn't that easy anymore. When we got to "Eddie's Camp," everyone was teasing me about how big I had gotten and guessing as to what I was having. It was all that usual stuff you hear when your pregnant. Eddie never really came over to me. He just stayed behind everyone else and watched which was unusual for Eddie because whenever we arrived, he was always so loud and yelling about something.

Finally, it seemed everyone was going their own ways, in their rooms to put food or clothes away and Alan and the others went to talk to some of the other workers. I was left pretty much alone, outside by the van. So I started to straighten out the things in the trunk knowing all along Eddie was there also watching me. After a few minutes, he started walking over towards me and all I heard was this loud "Hey!" I turned and said, "Eddie, Hey how you doing?" It was just small talk. He never answered the question. He just pointed at my belly and said "You sur' got big, Mrs. When you havin' that child, any ways?" I told him soon and that's why I wouldn't be able to come back to the camps for a while. I would be home taking care of the baby. So he made a kind of grunt noise like he understood and looked at me a while. He asked me "You be havin' a nigga' woman take care of you baby?" This shocked me! I said no, that I take care of my own children. With no real expression but in a very firm loud voice he told me "Don't move, stay right there." He started to walk to his room and just as he got to his weather beaten cracked door, he turned and yelled, "Don't move now, I mean it!" I nodded and said "Okay!" I had no idea what he was doing, so when he came back out of his room with a huge machete my heart really started to beat like I had just stepped off a treadmill. He didn't walk my way. He walked into the field saying "I'll be back Mrs. You say you wouldn't move! 'member that, now!"

A while later I saw him up by the packing pavilion, where the harvest was taken for cleaning, packing and shipping. He was doing something, but I couldn't see what it was. Then he started back up the road toward me. As he got closer he hung his machete in his belt behind him, which made me feel a lot better. He finally reached me and stood there with the biggest and most perfect head of cabbage I'd ever seen. Holding it out to me and with tears in his eyes and as soft as I had ever heard him speak, he said "take it, it for your Mrs. I love your Mrs. And have a good baby. God bless you now, hear!" At that moment, you could have knocked me over with a feather. I told him I would miss him and would keep him in my prayers. My heart was so overwhelmed, I felt as though someone had just given me the biggest and most perfect rose they could find, but this was better. Eddie gave what he could, and it had been picked and cleaned just for me by a man so many people feared and called crazy. Was he really crazy? Did he want to be that way? Or was it just survival - Eddie's way? All I know is it's hard sometimes to explain to people when they say why do you do it? Why waste your time going out to "these camps," "no one appreciates it, they'll survive - they always have." Some Christian people will sometimes quote the scriptures and say, "you know you shouldn't cast your pearls before swine." I'm sure this causes the Lord to weep. It's times like this, with Eddie, when you really get to see and understand that these are people, real people, people that have feelings and more importantly some still have dreams. Just because of a part of the country they grew up in or the way they grew up they should not suffer for it. They allow people to walk on them and use them, but it doesn't make it right. It's not right that they should fall through the cracks in our government whether it be town government or Washington DC. They need help! This kind of help could only prove to be good!

Migrant camps or labor camps whichever you choose to call them, are not at all good places. The people that live there may never be able to be mainstreamed into society, maybe they don't want to be - some are very happy right where they are. It is very important for the children of the workers to have a chance. If the children can be helped or the younger men and women, the chain can be broken, change will occur. As it did for Elsie and Slim.

Documentation Photographs

43

45

TEBL

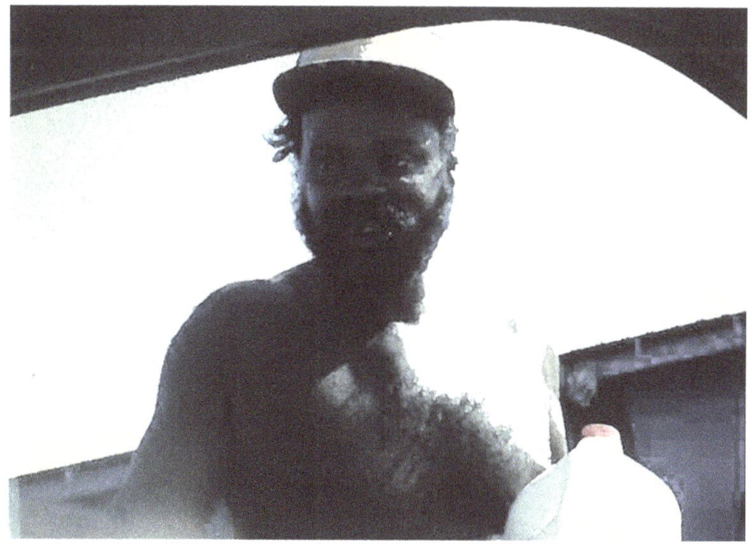

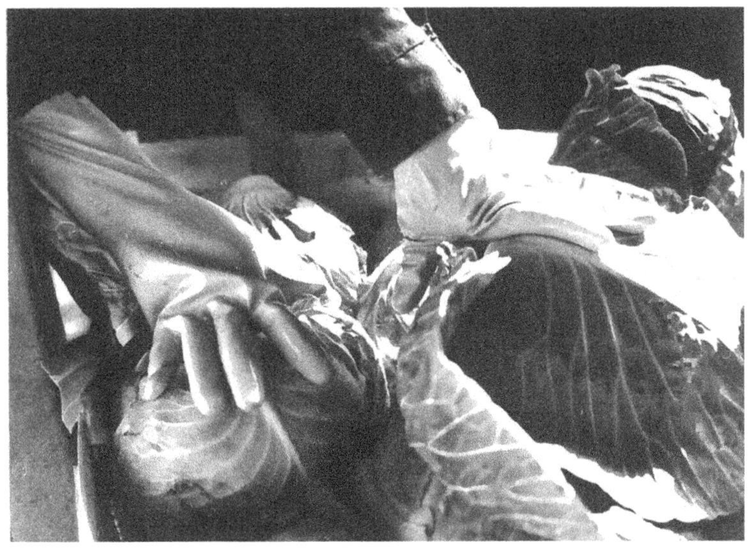

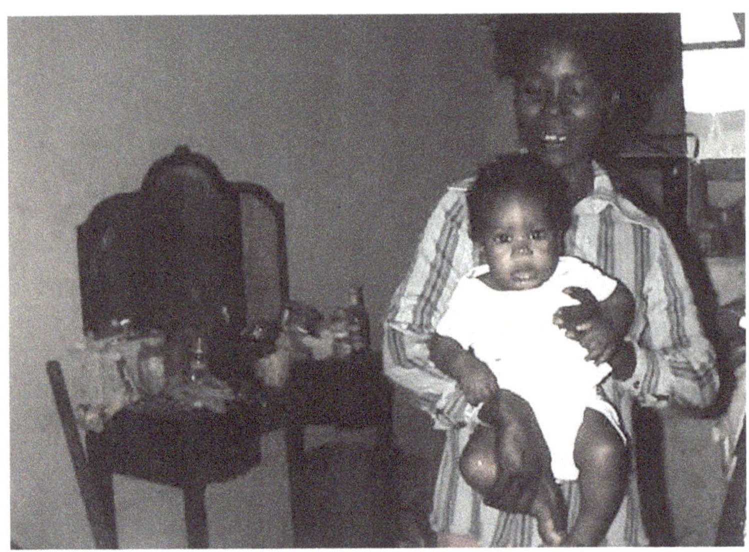

CHAPTER NINE

Slim and Elsie

I spoke earlier of Slim and his wife Elsie. Well, it didn't take too long and Slim got that old car running. So on days off, they would pack up their two sons and drive off, get away from the camp. I didn't realize at the time, but Elsie had two other older boys. They were living with their grandmother in another small town about an hour away. An hour away doesn't seem all that far, but when you live like Slim and Elsie, it may as well be a million miles away, because most times, they wouldn't have enough gas to go visit the boys. On special occasions, they would drive over and visit them. If someone from their town was coming to Lumbell, they would take the boys to visit them. Slim wasn't the boys' real father, but he loved them like his own. Their dad lived not all that far from the camps in a small two bedroom shack. It looked like one strong wind could blow it over. So most of the time if the boys were to come to visit, Elsie would have them stay with their real dad. She felt it was better than the camp. She was right.

It was around Thanksgiving time when we first met them. They were playing outside at their dad's, they were about five and six years old at the time. I could tell right away they were Elsie's kids.

One had that same shy smile as Elsie and he was thin and very dark, polite, very-welled mannered. Whenever you talked to him, he answered "yes ma'am or no ma'am." His name was Trevor. The other boy was one year younger than Trevor, about five - but a real spitfire. He was just as polite as his brother, but real boy. He couldn't sit still for a minute. He was built huskier, but just as dark as his brother. He name was William. They both had smiles that could light up the darkest of rooms. Their teeth were so white and perfect as could be, and they were adorable. Elsie was as proud as she could be of them, and had a right to be. She told me how well they did in school and how good they were for their grandmother.

When we knew that they were going to be at their dad's, we would be sure to stop in and give them whatever we had. Then Christmas came and we knew Elsie and Slim wouldn't be able to afford anything for the kids that year; after all, they were in debt like all the other workers. The strange thing was the kids weren't even expecting anything. There was really never even a mention of Christmas. No talk of Santa Claus, it was all just another day in the month to them.

Earlier that month through a Christian radio station, people heard about our little group and what we were doing and someone called and donated a truck to us. It was an old and faded-out truck, but it ran. Things started coming in left and right - after all it was Christmas time and that old man "guilt" was raising his ugly head.

Toys for Tots, a great organization by the United States Marine Corps, called us and asked if we knew of any migrant kids that could use some toys for Christmas. Boy, did we - and of course, we thought of Trevor and William first. At the time, we had about twenty to twenty five kids at the camps. We went and picked up teddy bears, trucks, dolls, cars, basketballs, baseballs and bats. If there were was a real Santa Claus, I knew exactly how he felt - GREAT! We also had turkeys for some who could cook and we took out dinners already prepared for all the workers. Friends of ours had donated time and energy to help put together all these dinners, all consisting of chicken, rolls, a hard boiled egg and vegetable. Boxes filled to overflowing, filled the truck to the point that it couldn't fit another thing; plus cars followed behind with more things. That day, the workers were waiting for us, but it was different than usual. It was Christmas Time! Even the feeling in the air was different. It was light, everyone seemed happy. Today, they were more patient with each other. Everyone was shaking hands and saying Merry Christmas. When we were done with the migrant camps and finished giving out their gifts of hats, gloves and socks, it was time to go to Trevor's and William's house. To everyone, this was what we were waiting for.

When we arrived at the small insignificant house, the boys were just sitting on the small railing on the front porch. We didn't realize right away, but they were waiting for us - news traveled real fast that day. They knew today was a special day. It was about four days before Christmas and we were celebrating early. They really still didn't expect a thing, but they waited. They wanted to see what was going to be so special. We got out of the truck and asked if their dad was home - he was - and he came out and so didn't about a half dozen other people we had never seen before. The focus was on the boys. We asked them if they wouldn't mind helping carry some stuff and they said sure. I guess they figured on more can goods and cereal. Ah! But today was going to be different! Today was pies and bright colored cookies all decorated in reds and green, and ribbon candy. Their eyes opened so big I thought they would pop. They asked if they could have one now. We told them of course they could if it was okay with their dad. It was. Their dad took the rest of the stuff in which include one of the turkeys with all the fixings and as he took it, all he could say was "thank ye all and bless you - bless you," and the tears rolled down his cheek. We told the boys to come around the back of the truck and we picked up a blanket which we were using to cover the real surprises. When the blanket was lifted, they couldn't believe what they saw. Presents all wrapped up in beautiful paper and bows with their names on them! They didn't know what to do. Alan called out their names and handed them their gifts. They just looked at each other waiting for the other one to react first. Then all at once, it all broke loose. They started yelling and jumping, some of the presents never quite made it inside. They just ripped them apart and if you could understand this, they hugged them. It's a sight I will never forget and a feeling that will never leave my soul.

The greatest part was to come, though I didn't realize it at the time. About a year later, Elsie and Slim got their dream come true. They moved off the camp. We helped with getting some furniture donated, sheets, towels and, of course, food to fill their new kitchen. Slim went to work for a plumber and Elsie worked in the big hotel in "Oz." It wasn't a glamorous job by no means. It was doing dishes, but it was a job. They were very happy, and the main thing was they were all together. We didn't see them much any more, only if we happen to see each other at the store or gas station. We made sure all was well, and it was. Elsie still had her dream of leaving Lumbell to see other places and her boys getting a good education and doing something with their lives, which did not include very doing farm work. We never saw the boys.

Time went on, actually about eights years of time!

My Heart

I got a job working in the school system in our county. I worked in the Middle School which included sixth, seventh, and eight grades. I enjoyed it. I liked being around the kids.

One of my duties during the day was sitting in the "in-school suspension room" better known as "ISS." It was the alternative to being suspended from school, or if a student was misbehaving in class, they were sent to ISS to just sit away from their regular class. The kids were to sit there with absolutely no talking, no turning around. They were to just do their school work. They got two bathroom breaks, one in the morning and one in the afternoon. They even ate their lunch in the ISS room. So it was pretty serious stuff when you get sent there. Needless to say, the kids hated it! It wasn't only boring for the kids but as you can image, it got very boring for us who had to sit with the little "inmates." So at times, we broke the rules a bit and struck up conversations.

This one particular day, I was sitting there as usual and in walked another student to add to the day's catch. Of course, just like all the rest, he wasn't very happy to be there. He signed in on the sheet that sat on my table without a word, and I told him where to sit and gave him a list of the rules, which basically said "only breathe when absolutely necessary." I told him to open his books to work. He never said a word - still he looked as though the whole world hated him. As I sat there I kept thinking "I know this boy from somewhere." There was nothing special about him really, he was in eighth grade, about 5'7" tall and had a big build. He was black and seemed like the quiet type. After about forty five minutes, I broke silence, and asked him what he did to get put in ISS. Well, when you ask one of these kids that question, look out - the can of worms is about so spill all over the place. As usual, it wasn't his fault, "the teacher man what a jerk," and "no on in this school likes me man, they're always disin' me!" Well, I listened and tried to assure him none of that was true. For whatever good it did, it did calm him down a bit. That's when I told him he looked real familiar to me and asked him where he lived. He told me he lived in Lumbell which didn't surprise me. The more we talked, the more I was sure I knew him. So I kept asking questions. I felt like I was giving him the third degree. Then it finally happened - the right question! I asked him if his parents worked on the labor camps out at the farms. He told me they used to "awhile back." I asked him which one and if he every lived there. He explained: "Me and my brother stayed with my real dad in a house down the road from the camp. My ma stayed with her old man Slim in the camp. She didn't want us there. She say it was a bad place for us, but my small brother stay out there with them. Slim's his real dad." Finally, the bottom line, the answer I was waiting for. Now I was getting somewhere. The bells in my head were going off. I felt so much excitement, it was like finding an old lost relative! I practically yelled Slim's name when I said, "Slim - 1 know him!" Then I said, "I know now, your mom is Elsie and you've got an Aunt Orlene married to Gerald!" The look on his face was shock and surprise. How did this white lady with this funny accent know so much about his family? So I told him how my husband and I would bring food and clothes out to the migrant camps on the weekends and pray with everyone if they wanted us to. He looked and looked for a while then finally he said, "the preacher man your ol' man?" I was so excited I said "Ya, the preacher man that's him!" Then came the blessing of my life. The thing that made it all worthwhile. The reason why we spent time sharing and giving our time so many times in the past eight years. He looked at me with his dark eyes starting to fill with tears and said "your ol' man used to drive a old truck kinda white color?" I had to think a minute, then the memory came back. The old truck he spoke of was the donated truck. Now I was shocked he remembered. He couldn't have been more than six or seven years old at the time. He began to tell me of his "Special Christmas." How he sat with his brother out on the small front porch of his dad's house. The memory came flooding back to me, along with tears in my eyes. What a blessing God had just given me.

I get a chance to tell him about his mother's dreams and how hard her and Slim worked to get them all to this point in their lives. I think it still shocked him a bit that I was able to tell him all about his family. Suddenly we weren't strangers any more, we became good friends!

Later that day, William had gotten out of ISS and my duty was also up for that day. I was now doing hall duty, when I heard William yell my name. I saw him down the hall practically dragging this other student. I just said, "William what on earth are you doing?" He had a big smile on his face, that could still light up a room, and said, "Ms. Rosanne, this is Trevor, 'member my brother? Hey Trev' this here is the preacher man's ol' lady - oh man! Sorry, Mrs. Rosanne - his wife - member Trev?" Trevor just stared and said "wow - I can't believe it, man - Thank You!"

Oh, if I was ever unsure of why we did everything we did for these people, the answer was in these two faces! Our friendship goes on - they're in high school now doing great. They play sports and very good I might add, and do pretty good with grades. The important thing is they have dreams and hope for the future. College is tops on their list and a big house and lots of money, just like any other kid! The difference is these two have seen how impossible dreams can come true and have been taught how to work hard for them!

CHAPTER ELEVEN

A Baby Herself

I've been greatly blessed to see the mighty miracle that happened in Slim and Elsie's life and the boys.

Still, I can never stop wondering and worrying about the workers we've met then and have moved on. They don't necessarily move on to better circumstances. At least in most cases that is what we have observed.

I often think of the young mother of a baby girl.

We heard that there were some workers in another part of Lumbell, even further out than the camps we were already visiting. It seemed like we had driven down this old dirt road for about ten miles. We almost gave up and turned around. Suddenly we saw some shacks up ahead. As we got closer, we would see that there were three houses. The main house was a big two-story house and probably in it's day, about 60 or 70 years ago, it was used as the "main" house for this particular farm. The smaller houses were probably used for slaves or workers. The "main" house was no longer livable. The floors has collapsed and everything was boarded up, and the roof was half gone. We were about to turn around and leave, but we finally had learned not to be as naive as Dorothy! So we snooped around outside a little. As we get closer to the smaller shack that we were sure no one could possibly live in, we heard a noise. We would see something or someone moving around through the cracks in the boards that kept this place together. So we went up to the door and knocked lightly on it for fear anything harder would have caused it to fall down. We stood there a while and waited before we knocked again; then we saw an eye looking through a crack in the door. We yelled in "hello, we don't mean to bother you, we just came to see if you need anything!" Still, nothing. Then we said, "the workers at the other farm sent us, we help them out now and then and they told us to see you. They said you might be in need of some things!" Finally, a reply. It was a soft, almost frightened voice of a young girl saying "my man he workin' he tell me neva' open da door to no one when he ain't here." We told her we didn't want her to do anything she didn't want to do. We could hear in her voice she was either real scared of us or her "man." It took a while of talk back and forth to finally win her confidence. She opened the door and we met face to face. Her face wasn't so different to us anymore. Her lip was swollen and her eye puffy enough to tell that same old story. She was tiny about 5'3" tall maybe 95 pounds when she was soaking wet, and she couldn't have been more than 16 or 17 years old.

She let me in. "Only fer' a minute you hear?" Alan went to the car for food and clothes. This so called house was unbelievable. Every wall I looked at I would see the outside. In one corner of the room, there was a whole big enough so that the cat jumped through and came in. I noticed on the other side of the room the corner was all closed in with rolled up rags and old towels on the floor. As I walked over, it was what I thought, a pile of dirty clothes. The young girl saw me looking and she came over quickly. She was smiling and with this proud look coming over her face, she said "that my baby, you wanta see, she pretty." I tried not to look so shocked when she reached into this mess and produced the cutest little new-born baby girl you ever saw. She had no crib so this mess on the floor was her bed. The holes in the walls on this side of the room were filled with old crumpled newspapers.

Alan had the food so we walked outside, plus we didn't want to overstay our welcome, although she was beginning to enjoy our visit. We asked her if we could come back. She said she would like it very much if we did. We told her we would try real hard to bring some things for the baby when we came back. We prayed with her before we left and with the prayers came tears. She stood in the doorway and waved as we drive away with a huge smile on her face.

My mind was already racing with thought of what church groups I could contact for help for our new found friend. The woman at the local Baptist church kept coming to mind. The next day, I called one of the woman at the church. She was great, she ran the out - reach ministry for the needy and was always ready to help. That very night, the women were having a meeting. At that meeting, they decided they would have a baby shower for the new mother and her baby. This would be a very unique shower, they would hold it without the mother and baby present. That's just what they did. The following week all the women came to their meeting with gifts all wrapped and baby food, formula and diapers. It was wonderful. All this was done and ready for delivery for a Sunday visit.

She was outside this time, and she saw us coming, and we could see her beautiful smile as we got closer. Her man was home this time, but she had told him all about us, so although he didn't smile right off, he wasn't hostile either. As we got out of the van, everyone was saying their hellos and this time she hugged us like we were family. Just like a kid at Christmas time, you could see her excitement as she tried to peek in the van unnoticed. We didn't make her wait or wonder for long, we were just as excited as she was. Alan went around the back of the van, unlocked it and threw it open. He said "Praise God," it's all for you and that baby of yours. She just stood there with her hands over her mouth and tears coming out of her big dark eyes. We told her how all the presents were collected and all about the Baptists women's group. She looked so surprised and said "why they do this fer' me? They don't know me or my baby?" We tried to explain to her that God was the "key" to it all. He put the burden in the hearts of these people to want to help her because he cares for them and that she is a very important person in God's eyes. As we started to empty the van, the excitement was even higher, even her "man" was teary eyed. After a while, we finally finished, we all said our goodbyes and they thanked us a hundred times. They also told us to pass thanks onto the Baptists women. We did happily!

We continued to visit the young family for a couple of months. Until one Saturday, we drove down the road as usual, pulled up in front of the little house, but it was very quiet. We called out, but got no answers back. We looked in through the cracked walls to see what we could. We noticed the door was partly opened so we went in. They were gone. There was nothing left except some old rags here and there, some empty cans of food.

We never heard from them or about them again. It's very hard when people move on this like, but this is how they work. I compared by feelings to how I guessed a foster mother feels after putting so much caring and giving into someone; then all at once, their out of your life. You wonder, if they'll get the help they need at the next place. Then you realize you have to just give it up to the Lord and keep praying for them!

The Bible tells us "trust in God for all things…" Not an easy scripture to live by sometimes.

CHAPTER TWELVE

Dave & Nancy

Labor camps in many cases are a hiding place for people. Sometime for people running from the law, or their country or families. In some case, just running from things their not even sure of.

Another couple we lost track of comes to mind. They were a young couple. He has in his early forties, she was in her thirties - at least that's what we guessed. Their names were Dave and Nancy. They were the only whites in the camp. No one seemed to mind, although when we first met them, one of the first things Dave said to us was "they're always watching us, can't trust any of em'." We ignored him. He sounded pretty paranoid to us. Most of the guys on the camp told us to watch him, they told us he was "crazy." Dave was an ex-marine but never used the past tense in describing himself as a marine, which we thought was a little strange. He had been in combat in Viet Nam, a war it seemed, he was still fighting.

Dave wasn't a real big guy, maybe about 5'9" or 10" tall, slim build, but his arms looked like he still worked out. He wore his black hair in that short GI style haircut. He always wore flip flop sandals and GI issued t-shirts with his dog tags hanging on the outside. I don't think there was ever time we saw him when he was completely sober. He drank heavily. His temper would rage if a word was ever mentioned about his drinking.

Nancy also drank very heavy, but she was opposite of Dave. She was very quiet. She was about 5'5" tall, her dark hair which she never combed straggled on her shoulders. She weighed all of 75 or 80 pounds, she literally was a walking skeleton. She always had dark circles under her eyes even when they weren't blackened by Dave's fist.

Whenever we went out to the camp that Dave and Nancy worked at, he would always go on and on about how he was going to own a pig farm in Virginia. Dave would tell us that any day now his brother would come for him and Nancy. We always let him go on about it never really paying much attention. We figured what really were the chances of this happening? A couple of the workers would tell him "shut up man, preacher man don't wanna hear you goin' on 'bout nonsense!" Well this got Dave angry to think we didn't believe him. We could see him beginning to light up like a firecracker ready to explode. So when he told us, "come on my ol' lady tell you - she don't lie." We followed him not wanting to get him any more angry. He took us to this room; which because they came late to the camp, they got what room was left. It was in the back of the building, it looked like it used to be some kind of patio porch. It had windows on two sides only half with glass, the others Dave had put plastic on them to keep out some of the weather. As we walked up to the room, I looked in through a window and saw a mattress on the damp cement floor. Not on the mattress, but next to it laid Nancy, her face was bruised and swollen and her left hand was all swelled out. Someone had broken two of her fingers. Dave walked in and pushed her with is foot to get her up. There was no way. She had drank so much I don't think she ever realized what shape she was in nor did she care. We convinced Dave to leave her and said we believed him. Told him we were interested in hearing all about his pig farm. This pacified him for a little while.

As we started to give out food to the others, he disappeared. We really didn't notice. We all noticed when he reappeared, literally dragging Nancy by her hair then holding her up by his arm with her head in a wrestler's head lock. Everyone was shocked to see this. A couple of the workers told us, "he crazy man, his mind no good now how." Alan handled the situation. Dave let a couple of the ladies take Nancy to another room to let her sleep it all off. When we got home that day, we called a couple of people who we thought could help. They did! They took Nancy to the women's shelter for two days - but Dave wanted her back. So when the crew chief found out where she was, he got her back for him. So Nancy went back to the camp. A couple of weeks passed. We went to the camp on a Saturday and found out by the workers a man and a lady in a truck came one day and picked Dave and Nancy up - they were going to their pig farm in Virginia.

I think of them often, especially Nancy. I wonder if she's alright, or if she's still alive. I pray they never have any children to witness what I have witnessed in their relationship.

CHAPTER THIRTEEN

Crew Chief

The crew chief or boss man in the migrant camps hold a lot of control over the workers. It isn't respect or admiration they have of his person. It's fear. They know he holds all the cards in some cases, although we really never witnessed it ourselves. He holds life and death over them. He feels he has ownership of them. The workers feel there really isn't anyone else in life that is all that interested in them or care about them. It's the end of the road.

We were at "Eddie's Camp" one day. I was standing out front of the building talking with some of the men. We just finished giving out hot coffee, orange juice and doughnuts. The boss man drove up and got out of his truck. All the workers stopped what they were doing and started towards him. One man actually went into one of the rooms and came out with an old chair, wiped it off with the sleeve of his shirt and said to the boss man "here you go sir, sit, you rest now." Rest, you have to be kidding me, I wanted to scream! He had come to see if you wanted to do some work on another farm for the day. Naturally, they all raised their hands and he picked who exactly he wanted.

I'm sure he was getting paid pretty good that day, so he wanted to show off his best workers. I never found out what the workers got that day for working.

Sometimes it's very hard to find out what any of the workers really make for a wage. I did see a couple of the mens' pay one day. They never get paid by check, always by cash and on the envelope of the pay will have the amount they still owe the crew chief and what's in the envelope. The crew chief is paid by the farmer who hired the crew chief and his workers. When the law people from South Florida were at the farms, there was an investigation of the books of one of the crew chiefs, but it was also explained to me how he keeps two books. One to show if anyone should ask to see them and one actual one that he really uses. In all our years helping migrants and all the injuries at the camps we have seen, the workers receive from working in such bad conditions, never have we seen any one of them collect workmen compensation, or retire and collect a social security check. Yet there are many over sixty two years old. Does anyone check into any of this? Are inspectors really that naive or do they really not see any of this going on?

CHAPTER FOURTEEN

Pablo

The migrant workers were late coming back one season, real late. It was already late November and there was no sign of them. Alan and I would take drives out periodically to check on them, but there was no sign of life at all.

Finally, one day word got to us that there had been an accident.

The workers were on their way to Lumbell, when they met with a tractor trailer truck in their path. The driver of the truck didn't see the bus and when he did, it was too late to stop. The bus overturned and landed into a ditch. There were about 35 or 40 workers in the bus at the time. They were returning from their work in North Carolina. When the bus finally rested on its side, those who could, climbed out, those who couldn't waited for help. Workers told us that you could hear everyone screaming and moaning throughout the bus. When help did arrive it was very difficult to get at the people inside because of all their belongings. The workers never have suitcases so when they move from place to place, they just take what they can carry in their arms. So there were old clothes, blankets, dirty boots thrown everywhere, and on top of everyone.

The rescuers did the only thing they cold do. They got into the bus and started throwing things out the bus until they found who was left inside.

One of the people they found was Pablo. He was full blooded Apache Indian. He was in his mid 50's, about 5'8" tall, he had a stocky build. His skin was a deep reddish brown. He wore his hair long, a little bit past his shoulders and always wore an Indian head band across his forehead. Pablo wasn't at all the way TV stereotypes the Apache Indians. He was very quiet and a very gentle man. When we met him, we all immediately liked him. My husband Alan and Pablo got to be good friends right away. Also he was a very hard worker.

In the bus accident, he ended up with a broken arm and leg and a broken pelvis bone. He was in the hospital a very long time before he came back to the camp. When he did arrive, everyone was real glad to see him. He couldn't work like he did before but they did manage to give him other little things to do. Pablo really didn't understand what was going on about the accident, but the crew chief had started a law suit against the truck driver and his company. The suit took months, but finally came to an end. When it did, along with it came checks to all that had gotten hurt. Pablo also was awarded a check for $10,000 - more money than he could ever had imagined. He didn't read or write so when the check came, he was told by the crew chief to put his mark on the back of this check and also some papers he had. Being the trusting person Pablo was, he did just what he was told to do. The boss man told him he would take care of it all and that Pablo wouldn't have to worry about it when he needed anything. The money would be there. Pablo had told us about all of this. So in turn, we told the law people about it. They then spoke to Pablo about it and advised him to test the crew chief. He was told to tell him he wanted the money, he wanted to leave the camp and go home.

The next morning, Pablo did just that. To his surprise, the crew chief yelled at him, started to say, "who do you think you are boy, who takes care of you, who feeds you, no one cares about you, just me." Then the truth - he told him "there ain't no money, you used it all up boy, don't be asking me for no money." Pablo was shocked and very hurt. This also scared him, he didn't like to get the boss man mad at him. He liked to keep things quiet. The law people came back and he told them all about what happened. They were not surprised at all. So they drew up some papers that would get the crew chief in trouble and possible jail time. All Pablo had to do was put his mark on the papers. He couldn't do it. He later told us he was very afraid to do something like this. He said he was afraid the boss man would get so mad that we would never see Pablo again. He said as he pointed to the woods at the edge of the fields, "boss man take me out there and you'll never see me again, I don't need any money anyway."

The money was never mentioned again by us or by Pablo. Things went on as always - unfortunately.

CHAPTER FIFTEEN

Ruby

About 5' tall, very tiny built black woman, looked about ten years younger than she really was - her name is Ruby! She is one of our oldest friends from the camps we have. The first time we met her, she didn't come outside, she watched from a window downing her MD. When she finally did come out, it was to yell at us about everything and nothing. "Who you all think you are, comin' here to feed the nxxxx, what you got fer me?" We just stared at her, we knew she was drunk so we figured we'd just let her rave on, and she did!

Ruby lived with a young man, a man about 18 years her junior. His name was Hamp. He was a big guy, very quiet. They had been together for some time now. Their relationship was pretty much like all the other couples on the camp. They never actually got married, but in Florida after you've been together for seven years, your considered married. Most of the time, they were good to each other and were treated pretty good by the crew chief. Hamp was one of his top workers and Ruby was one of his top woman. She worked harder than some of the men on the camp. Her mouth so it seemed was as big as her entire being. When she was drunk and yelling you could hear her even before she got out the building.

One day at the camp, we came face to face. She started mouthing off to me, telling me we never bring her nothing, we don't like her, we're prejudice all that good stuff. So in turn I asked her what she wanted, what did she need - we'd get it. It didn't take her long with an answer, "I want me a real nice jacket, somethin' new, and I wants it to fit me!" So I said yes, I told her to pray for it because if she got it, it truly would be a gift from God. She gave a snicker, and walked away saying under her breath, "sure you all gonna get Ruby her jacket, we'll see." I felt in my heart this was something we really needed to happen to win this person over and for her to trust us. She was different than most of the workers, she had so much hate inside of her it scared me.

The next couple of days more clothes came in for the migrants, and each time we got things I went through the bags looking for that special jacket for Ruby. Nothing. Bag after bag and no jacket. I even tried calling around to different girls I knew that I felt were her size, asking them if they could donate - nothing! It got to where I was getting very worried about it, what was I going to tell her? It was Friday and we were going out to the camps on Saturday. I prayed - Oh God please help! Small prayers said with a full heart sometimes are the best prayers said. It was late Friday afternoon, when the phone rang. It was a friend of mine that I hadn't heard from in a very long time. She said she had heard that we were working with the migrant workers bringing them clothes and food. She said she had some things she would like to donate - could she bring them over - they were all clean and folded. I said sure, we would always use good clothes. We got a lot of things donated but about 50 percent of it had to be thrown away in the garbage.

It was about an hour later and my friend arrived with all her clothes to donate. They were all wonderful things, and the clothes she had that had been hers would fit ruby perfect. I thought maybe this would satisfy her. I thanked my friend and she was about to leave, and she stopped. She forgot one more thing. She pulled a near brand new lady's leather jacket out the back seat of her car and held it up. Do you think someone could use this she said. It was mine and I never wore it, it's just been sitting in my closet. Tears came to my eyes, and I told her the story of Ruby. She started to cry, what a miracle had just happened. It was wonderful. She left and I took everything inside. I showed Alan the jacket, he couldn't believe it. I knew I had to do something special with it, so I got a box and pretty wrapping paper and wrapped it all up and put Ruby's name on it.

The next day, like all other Saturdays, we were on our way to the camps. Today, though was different for me. I couldn't wait to get to Ruby's camp. Sure enough as we pulled up to her camp there she was waiting for us. We did as we always did, handed out the food and clothes to everyone, and while we did, Ruby stayed back never coming forward. Then Alan started to pray which usually everyone knew the food and clothes were all given out then. Except this time, it was different - there were still some special clothes and one beautiful box waiting under the seat. So I pulled it out and called for Ruby. She came towards the van saying, "what you all want, ain't nothin' fer me." I walked towards her and handed her the box and told her, "I guess God really thinks you're special because he got this just for you." She stood there a few seconds and for once in her life she didn't know what to say. She was actually quiet! All the other workers stood there in silence waiting for her to open the box. She finally started to take the paper off the box trying not to rip it. She got to the box and opened it. When she saw what was in it, she screamed and grabbed the jacket out of the box saying, "this is really fer me, only fer Ruby? Praise Jesus you all I love you!" The jacket fit her like it was made just for her - but I guess in a way - it was!

After that day, things changed between Ruby and me. We developed a good friendship. She never demanded anything from us. If she was in need, she would always ask us "if it be possible." She even started to take care of one of the elderly workers in the camp we all called Uncle Sam. She made sure he ate regular and tried to keep him from drinking so much. Ruby herself didn't stop drinking but did cut down. She was the only worker we ever gave our telephone number to, we trusted her. As time went on, she and Hamp moved off the camps. She even started to go to classes for her GED. She is doing fairly well. We see her now and then. We think of her always. She's a survivor so she will be an over comer!

CHAPTER SIXTEEN

Church isn't a Building

There was the camp we liked to call the church camp. This camp was a real mix of people. Also quite a lot of women and children. Whenever we would go to the "church camp," the women would all run inside and come out in seconds with their broken down old chairs or anything else they could sit on. Some would even have their Sunday best on including hats. If they had any kind of bible or prayer book, it was tucked in their arms and brother they were ready for church. They would all sit there and say, "brother Alan or Brother Carlos or Maurice preach it today, we all did have a hard week." They loved to hear the word of God. So the guys always made sure when we were going to this camp they were prepared. It was a sight to see all seven to ten women in Sunday best - maybe a bright plaid polyester pants suit with a flowered blouse that someone decided they did not want anymore and a pair of flip flops or old slippers on their feet. They would be shouting their amens and praises to the Lord… it was great. This camp was a little different probably because it had more women. When they were able to get food stamps regardless of how little they would pool them and give them to the cook and she would do the shopping and the cooking for everyone. The cook was a good and honest woman. She had an old trailer that she stayed in with her kids and where she did all the cooking for the entire camp. So even when we brought stuff to this camp, we gave a lot of it in bulk to her especially if anything got donated in large restaurant amounts. Then we gave the workers smaller things for them to have of their own.

Everything seemed to run pretty smoothly on this camp. It was run by a son of a bigger crew chief from another county. Everyone called him "Jitterbug." He drove a brand new candy apple red corvette and when he smiled which was most of the time, the first thing you would notice was the gold cap that covered his front tooth with "J" carved out of it. We always were a little surprised of all of the this, but the boss man always made it quite clear that if he wanted, he could see to it we never got on the farm to "his people" again if too many questions were asked. We never wanted that to happen. But what went on over the phones after we got home he never had to know. We made sure the inspector always had enough reasons to go out and inspect the camp.

This started to be the only way the county inspector could check the labor camps during the seasons. He would have to receive a formal complaint by phone or by letter from a member of the community. The county always claimed there was not enough money for wasted trips out to the labor camps.

Things started to get a little stranger than usual at the church camp. Everyone was acting differently when we saw them. The little joy we used to see in them was almost gone. There was more drinking at night. So much so, that one night one of the guys left his hot plate going to keep his room warm and burned down the trailer. He died in the fire, but thank God no one else did.

We explained all of this to the legal people, so they took a little trip out to make a visit. It didn't take them long to find out what was going on. Soon after their visit, the camp was closed down for all kinds of health violations and building code violations. Arrests were made of the crew chief and some good friends for selling cocaine and alcohol.

Everyone from the camp went in different directions. Some went to live in town with friends, some went back on the road and just started to walk. Most went to "Sammy's Camp." When he heard what was happening, he came to the rescue being such a good and caring guy that he was. He loaded the workers that were left and brought them all over to his camp and told his workers to make room, double and triple up if they had to. More workers meant more money in his pocket and there was no way a crew chief would pass that up.

As I have said, the labor camps are somewhat of a haven for all kinds of people. A haven for people running from everything and anything. We met people who were running from the law, wives, children, jobs. Yes, even jobs.

One man that comes to mind is Benjamin. We met him one Sunday at Eddie's camp. He never came out with the other workers. He just kind of stayed back and just listened, but we always knew he was there. My husband had put some stuff aside for him just in case he was in need. So when everything was given out and prayer was over, as usual we would just stand around and talk to everyone. This time, Alan went over to Benjamin and introduced himself and told him about our little group. He gave him the bag he had made up for him. You could see how glad Benjamin was to get it. He was the same as all the rest. He arrived at the camp with just what he had on his back. The bag had some food in it, soap, razors, a washcloth, toothbrush and toothpaste. They way he looked at it you might think Santa Claus just came. Alan and Benjamin talked a while. Alan did most of the talking. Before we left, we asked Benjamin if there was anything he might want special or anything he might be interested in to read. We liked to have the guys be able to do something besides drink when they were bored and work was slow. Well, to our surprise, he said he liked computers and asked if we had magazines about computers. Well, in all our time with the migrants, that was the first time we ever had one request something on such a subject as computers. We knew something had to be up with this guy and we were sure the story was going to be interesting. But for now, the story was going to have to wait, this was not the time to ask him. We had to give him time to trust us. He still seemed a little uncomfortable. We told him his request for the magazines shouldn't be very hard to fill. We had a lot of friends that worked at ITT and did a lot of work with computers, so they had to have some hanging around somewhere. Also as soon as we got home, I made some phone calls, and in a couple of days, we had enough magazines and books on computers to start a small library! Some of the other workers - being nosey as usual - wanted to see the books and started teasing Benjamin, saying "What you doin' man you gonna do school - you gonna be some big man-shooot." They would laugh folding in half, banging into each other as if they had to hold each other up! Benjamin was happy to get the magazines and books and ignored the others workers and took everything into his room. One of the workers came to Alan and told us that all Benjamin did was stay to himself in his room. He said "he don't talk to nobody brodder Alan, you need to talk to dat boy - sommin' ain't right, you hear what I'm sayin?" Just as he said that, Benjamin came walking back out and headed right to Alan. You could tell by the look on his face we were about to hear the secret, or at least Alan was going to hear it. He asked Alan if he could speak to him on the side and to the side of the building they went. And did he have a story to tell.

As it happened, he arrived at the camp about a week before we actually met him. He got here by bus like most of the others guys. The bus had picked him up on the outskirts of Jacksonville, Florida, which seemed about a million miles away to him right now. The day he got picked up, he had just walked out of his $45,000 computer job. He said he had gotten to a boiling point and couldn't take the stress any longer and left. He said he just got up from his desk and walked out of the building. He took off his suit jacket and threw it away with his tie and kept walking right down the street. He wasn't sure how far he had walked but got tired and saw some guys loading a bus and just did the same. Kind of like sheep.

The ride wasn't a long one, only about one and a half hour. When he was getting off, he was a bit shaken and scared, and not at all sure where he was or what was expected of him. He had no money; the wallet he figured had gotten stolen along the way, but wasn't about to ask anyone about it. He did know he needed help! So when we came along, he knew this was his chance. He wanted to go home. He knew nothing could be worse than the past few weeks he had just spent in this hell hole. So, of course Alan told him we would help him get out. He made some phone calls since no one in his family knew where he was. Needless to say, they were very happy to hear from him. Within two days, he was gone. It left us with a great feeling to help someone get out and to where they truly belong.

There have been a few along the way. One sweet guy hadn't been home for about 20 years, said he used to be a trumpet player with Bebe King and went bad on drinking and drugs. He was ashamed and just never went back home again or played again. He played for us, and he was good. We got him a one way but ticket back home. He wrote to us a while later and told us how happy he was and that he could die happy now that he was home again.

The feeling we get when this happens is just undescribable. It's great!

CHAPTER SEVENTEEN

MIGRANT CAMPS – LABOR CAMPS – HELL HOLES

Whatever you call them the smell is the same! It's funny when you think we live in a world that technology has changed and grown so much. We live in a country that with every year thrives and get stronger and more powerful. Our government officials have aided in tearing down the Berlin Wall, putting an end to communism in Russia and ending Apartheid in South Africa.

We send hundreds of thousands of dollars to underdeveloped countries, and rebuke those country leaders for treating their own people they way they do.

Yet here in this great country, we sit and do nothing about places that still exist like labor camps. If you think about it, if jails were run like labor camps, where the inmates would riot and the government would see that things got changed. But in labor camps, it's different. It is literally a place where no law presides over and where survival of the fittest reigns.

When my grandparents came to this wonderful country from Italy, they saw the Statue of Liberty for what she really stood for. Liberty and justice for all and protection. Yet, we still have migrants that come here and hide in labor camps and do anything they are told to for fear they won't be able to share in the great American dream. I believe if people are willing to endure what they do to stay here, they deserve to stay and be protected. To be given the chance to live out their dream that so many others had before them.

It's a sin to find a Mexican mother in a one room shack with no running water and only one light bulb hanging from the ceiling for electricity. While her husband works the fields, she hides her children for fear she'll be found out and deported. This fear is usually put there by a crew chief to keep them working hard and to keep them on his farm.

When you meet these people, one of the first things you notice is the look on their faces. It's that of no hope. If a man has no hope, he has nothing, he is merely a shadow in life, never being really whole, or feeling fulfilled.

As people, never mind Americans, we should be ashamed and embarrassed that towns like Lumbell Florida and Vidal Texas still exist. Where the N word is still used. America throughout history has been a great melting pot, where all races, religions and colors come together. Maybe they did not always get along, but after time, they would learn. So does this mean people are getting more stupid, more ignorant as time goes on!

Recently, my youngest daughter in the fourth grade got an assignment in school to write an essay on "What would Martin Luther King's dream now?" She asked my opinion and we talked about it a while. After talking about different things that happen in the United States and the world today, she came to the conclusion, as I did, that unfortunately his dream would have to be the same. For all men to be free and all men regardless of the color of their skin would learn to live together as brothers and sisters.

We have such a long way to go. The United States aided in ending communism yet, here at home, we have youth that march with the swastika proudly following the rule of a dead man. The United States aided in ending Apartheid in South Africa, yet here at home we still; have grown men marching in the street of the south with white sheets covering them, called the Klu KLux Klan, KKK or "The Klan." We can't forget our newest hate group, the Skin Heads which is growing in numbers all over our country. More youth yelling white power. How awful it must be to walk down the street and hate almost everyone you pass. They hate Blacks, Spanish, Jews - I guess just about everyone that doesn't blush! I'm not quite sure there is any real thing as "pure white" anymore. Remember, we're the melting pot! Family trees go back real far now. It's no longer one or two limbs on a branch, it's hundreds. Are all these so called white pure babies sure they're so snow white! Maybe some of them should check a little closer as to where some of their black or brown hair came from or their brown eyes. And where did some of our Black brothers and sisters get some of their green and blue eyes from! Just some food for thought.

As you can see, I have a little bit of a problem with people who don't except other people strictly because of what color their skin is or what religion or race they are. When a person is born, do they have a choice of these things? Of course not. But they do have a choice to hate and what a waste of life to hate all day, every day. It is such a waste of energy!

I remember when I was very young and the Rev. Martin Luther King, Jr. was alive, my parents along with the priest from our church, Father Goyna, went to a peace march. Our priest fought very hard against racism. He believed in Martin Luther King and President Kennedy's stand against it. The march was held in the city next to our town, which I might add our town only had one Black family in it. There were hundreds and hundreds of people that night standing in the park behind the city hall. Some people lit candles, there were speakers who spoke on the wrongs of racism. Towards the end, everyone held hands and sang songs. It was a wonderful thing to witness. Even at that young age I would feel how right all this was, I really couldn't understand what the big deal was anyway, wasn't this the way grown-ups were suppose to act?

My first real bout with prejudice came personally to me in high school. I had a very good friend in school and out of school. I lived in one part of town and she lived in the other. Well, where I lived was always considered the Italian section, which was true. My neighborhood was mostly Italians and I think I was related to 3/4 of them. My friend came from the part of town which was considered the WASP country (White Anglo Saxon Protestants). The war over this had been raging longer than the Hatfields and the McCoys. Being friends, we never even thought about it, until one night. We had both gone out to the movies. She had asked me to spend the night at her house when we got back. She had been to mine many times. Little did I know, she lied to her parents when she came to mine. When we got home, her mom called her to her bedroom to talk. Well, the talk got pretty loud. I could hear every word. My friend was being yelled at for having me sleep over, not because it was last minute or anything like that, but because it was me! The words burned through me, "How could you let that girl into our house to sleep in our beds! Those people are trouble and she's a hussy." "THOSE PEOPLE" - the words cut like a knife. I couldn't move, I didn't know what to do, and it scared me! She made me sound so dirty, and bad. Yet I was proud to be who I was. My father always said jokingly, "there's only two kinds of people in the world - Italians and those who wish they were Italian!" Needless to say, our friendship didn't last too much longer after that night. Some times, when I think of her, I hope she is married and is happy, but I also hope she married a very dark half - Italian, half Puerto Rican guy. I can laugh now but I know how I felt and that feeling will never leave me. But I also can't imagine feeling like that every day. Always thinking, knowing around every corner people hate you for a reason you cannot do anything about, and wouldn't want to change anyway. The pride a person feels about themselves has to go beyond their own neighborhoods. How else can you cope with the outside world. You have to be able to believe in yourself and know you matter, you count for something in this life.

SO... no, Doctor King, your dream has not come to life yet, in some aspects maybe, but not in most.

It was only this week that I heard a little four-year old black girl yell something to her friend at a day care center that confirmed to me the way I feel about all of this. It saddens me beyond words.

The little black girl had a stuffed animal she was letting her friend play with. A little white boy walked up to them and wanted to see the stuffed animal and was trying to touch it. With all the rage and anger, a four year old can muster, the little black girl yelled "Hey, don't let that white boy touch my toy - go away white boy - go away we don't play with no red neck boy!" He looked at the both of them and as young as he was hew knew enough to just walk away that he wasn't where he was suppose to be.

Another instance in the very same week at the same day are center. A five year old little white boy, wearing cowboy boots, with his little thumbs tucked into his front pockets of his jeans, looked straight up at his day care worker as bold as could be and said "My mama told me I don't have to listen to no nxxxx lady" and walked away!

When I hear these things, my heart sinks and a hurt comes into me that I really can't explain, but I do know that if more people had this feeling, maybe they would change.

I can't imagine any parent consciously teaching their child such horrifying morals. Teaching them in this day and age that another human being is a lower form of life than them.

Our culture in the United States comes from a mixture of cultures from all over the world. Our music, such as Jazz, Blues, Rap even the Big Band sounds. How can someone listen to all of this and say they hate Blacks, very contradictory. How about foods Americans love - Chinese, Mexican, Italian, Soul food, but they say they hate Asians, Spanish - another big contradictory. But yet without all of these different cultures, where would we be? What kind of televisions, stereos, cameras, computers would we have? You could go on and on with what all the different cultures bring together in this great country. Sometimes you should just try sitting down thinking about it for a while.

AUTHOR'S WORDS

As a second-generation American with Italian heritage, I owe much to the resilience and warmth of my family. My grandparents bravely crossed the Atlantic in search of a better life, enduring laborious jobs to provide for their family. My parents, though they never completed high school, were the epitome of wisdom, love, and pride—qualities they imparted to me alongside the most comforting embraces.

This book is a tribute to their legacy and the values they instilled in me: generosity, compassion, and the importance of withholding judgment, as we can never fully comprehend another's life story.

Thank you for taking the time to read my work. I hope it has broadened your perspective in some way.

With gratitude,

Rosanne Elworthy

A simple Italian girl from Massachusetts

"Sea of Green"

In conclusion, I must add that people have to stop looking at each other with color first. Stop seeing each other as threats instead of just people, plain and simple. It all goes back to the golden rule doesn't it? Do unto others as you would have them do unto you. But instead of still teaching this in the school today, we are taking this teaching out and trying to come up with new ways of teaching our kids. But it's not working. My mother always said sometimes the best things are right in front of your nose and you can't see it. If we don't wake up soon, all we are going to do is to teach our children how to destroy each other. As Americans we should be going forward, not backward. We should be setting the standard for other countries to follow, not for them to laugh at.

WE SHOULD NO LONGER HAVE SUCH PLACES AS LABOR CAMPS...